Victorian Factories

D0625068

Leabharlainn nan Eilean Siar

SY

WESTERN ISLES LIBRARIES

Readers are requested to take great care of the books while in their possession, and to point out any defects that they may notice in them to the Librarian.
This book is issued for a period of twenty-one days and should be returned on or before the latest date stamped below, but an extension of the period of loan may be granted when desired.

DATE OF RETURN	DATE OF RETURN	DATE OF RETURN
28. APR. 1999	21. JUN. 2002	12 OCT. 2011
11. SEP. 1999	10. OCT. 2002	1.3 APR. 2013
	14. DEC. 2002	-7 SEP 2017
41. OCT. 1999	10. OCT. 2003	11. 10. 18
	-2. APR. 2004	
26. OCT. 2000	25. JUN. 2004	
SESS 17	-9. OCT. 2004	
-8. FEB. 2001	30. MAR. 2007	
BACK		
-8. DEC. 2001		
23. MAR. ?AG	-3. MAY 2007	
	10 SEP 2011	

WITHDRAWN

WESTERN ISLES
LIBRARIES
39876805 J

J941.081

Andrew Langley

Illustrated by James Field

J941.081
39876805 J

Heinemann

WITHDRAWN

HISTORY OF BRITAIN – VICTORIAN FACTORIES
was produced for Heinemann Children's Reference
by Lionheart Books, London.

Editors: Lionel Bender, Sue Reid
Designer: Ben White
Editorial Assistant: Madeleine Samuel
Picture Researcher: Jennie Karrach
Media Conversion: Peter MacDonald
Educational Consultant: Jane Shuter
Editorial Advisors: Andrew Farrow, Paul Shuter

Production Controller: David Lawrence
Editorial Director: David Riley

First published in Great Britain by Heinemann Children's Reference,
an imprint of Heinemann Educational Publishers, Halley Court,
Jordan Hill, Oxford OX2 8EJ, a division of Reed Educational and
Professional Publishing Limited.

MADRID ATHENS
FLORENCE PRAGUE WARSAW
PORTSMOUTH NH CHICAGO SAO PAULO MEXICO
SINGAPORE TOKYO MELBOURNE AUCKLAND
IBADAN GABORONE JOHANNESBURG KAMPALA NAIROBI

© Reed Educational & Professional Publishing Ltd 1996

All rights reserved. No part of this publication may
be reproduced, stored in a retrieval system, or transmitted
in any form or by any means, electronic, mechanical,
photocopying, recording, or otherwise without either the
prior written permission of the Publishers or a licence
permitting restricted copying in the United Kingdom issued
by the Copyright Licensing Agency Ltd, 90 Tottenham
Court Road, London W1P 9HE.

ISBN 0 600 58929 3 Hb ISBN 0 600 58962 5 Pb

British Library Cataloguing-in-Publication Data.
A catalogue record for this book is available from
the British Library.

Printed in Italy

Acknowledgements

All artwork by James Field, except maps by Stefan Chabluk.

Photo credits Pages 4-5 (top): Bridgeman Art Library/City of Bristol
Museum & Art Gallery. 5 (centre): Mary Evans Picture Library/Illustrated
London News. 5 (bottom): Bridgeman Art Library/Wallington Hall,
Northumberland. 6 (centre left): Mary Evans Picture Library/ Illustrated
London News. 6 (top): Mary Evans Picture Library/ 'The Graphic' magazine.
7 (top): Bridgeman Art Library/Guildhall Library, Corporation of London
(detail). 7 (bottom): Billie Love Historical Collection. 8-9 (top): Gladstone
Pottery Museum, Stoke-on-Trent. 8 (centre left, bottom): The Mansell
Collection. 9: Mary Evans Picture Library/ 'English Illustrated' magazine.
10 (centre): Mary Evans Picture Library. 10 (bottom): Billie Love Historical
Collection. 11 (top): National Trust Photographic Library/Andreas von
Einsiedel. 11 (centre): Bridgeman Art Library/Manchester City Art Galleries.
11 (bottom): The Mansell Collection. 12: Hulton Deutsch Collection.
13 (top left, right): The Mansell Collection. 13 (centre): Bridgeman Art
Library/Guildhall Library, Corporation of London. 13 (bottom): Mary Evans
Picture Library. 14 (bottom left, right): The Mansell Collection. 14 (top),
15 (top): Hulton Deutsch Collection. 15 (right): Mary Evans Picture Library.
16 (top): Bridgeman Art Library/Forbes Magazine Collection, New York.
16 (bottom left) Gladstone Pottery Museum, Stoke-on-Trent. 16 (bottom
right): The Mansell Collection. 17: Hulton Deutsch Collection. 18 (top,
bottom): The Mansell Collection. 18 (centre): The National Museum of
Labour, Manchester. 19: Mary Evans Picture Library/ 'Illustrated London
News'. 20 (top left, bottom): Mary Evans Picture Library. 20 (top right):
Topham Picture Library. 21 (left): Bridgeman Art Library/Trades Union
Congress, London. 21 (right): The Mansell Collection. 22 (left): Hulton
Deutsch Collection. 22 (right): Robert Opie.

Cover: Artwork by James Field. Photographs: Tea caddy illustration of a
British company with plantations in Ceylon - Robert Opie. Children making
matchboxes - The Mansell Collection. Trade emblem - Bridgeman Art
Library/Trades Union Congress, London.

PLACES TO VISIT

Here are some sites and museums about Victorian industry
for you to visit. Your local tourist office will be able to tell you
about other places in your area.

Blists Hill Open-air Museum, Telford, Shropshire. A living
Victorian town, complete with iron works and blast furnace.

Bradford Industrial and Horses at Work Museum,
Yorkshire. This huge treasury of exhibits includes a spinning
mill, a mill-owner's house and workers' cottages.

Coalisland Corn Mill, County Tyrone. Museum of industrial
archaeology, with relics from (among other things) a
weaving factory.

Derwentcote steel furnace, Durham. The earliest steel
furnace. It fell into disrepair after it closed in the 1870s but
has now been restored.

Dock Museum, Barrow-in-Furness, Cumbria. Shows how
ships were built in Victorian times.

Long Shop Museum, Leiston, Suffolk. One of the very first
factory production lines used to build steam engines.

Maritime and Industrial Museum, Swansea, West
Glamorgan. A working woollen mill is among the many
exhibits.

New Lanark Visitor Centre, Lanark. Robert Owen's 'model'
town for his workers, with many restored houses and
machines on show.

North of England Open-air Museum, Beamish, Tyne and
Wear. Re-creation of an industrial town at the very end of
the Victorian era.

Port Sunlight Heritage Centre, Merseyside. A 'model'
village built by an idealistic soap manufacturer for his
workers in the 1880s.

Quarry Bank Mill, Styal, Cheshire. Galleries and preserved
cotton mill showing how workers and apprentices lived in
the 1830s.

Wigan Pier, Lancashire. Lancashire working life in 1900, as
performed by actors.

INTRODUCTION

Britain's 'factory age' began around 1750. The population was growing fast, which increased the demand for food, cloth and other goods. To meet this demand, new machines and processes were developed. Steam-powered looms turned out cloth faster than ever before. Coal furnaces produced better iron and steel, which hammers and rollers shaped into tools, rails and more machines.

All this changed the landscape and the way people lived and worked. Factories were built to house the machines. New towns sprang up around them. By the time Queen Victoria came to the throne in 1837, Britain was already a powerful industrial nation. During her 63-year reign, British industry reached its all-time high.

CONTENTS

FACTORIES AND FOUNDRIES

"From this foul drain the greatest stream of human industry flows out to fertilize the whole world." This is how a French visitor in the 1840s saw Manchester, one of the centres of Britain's cotton trade.

Factory towns like Manchester were dirty and unhealthy places. Yet the goods made there were sold all over the world and brought great wealth to Britain. In 1837, British exports earned nearly £44 million. By 1880 the total was over £218 million.

The most valuable export was cotton cloth, produced mainly in the mill towns of Lancashire and central Scotland. These were near the big ports such as Liverpool, where raw cotton arrived from the United States of America.

▽ **Smoke billows from the chimneys of a factory town in the 1870s.** In time, smoke grime covered the streets and the workers' cramped houses. Factory hands rush to work. Their homes were close to the mills, so public transport was not needed. Raw materials and coal for the factory were brought in by canal boats, horse-drawn carts or steam trains.

Coalfields
Iron ore fields

Fife
Ayrshire
Northumberland & Durham
Cumberland
Yorkshire
Lancashire
Derbyshire
Nottinghamshire
West Midlands
South Wales

△ **The main industrial areas of Britain in 1848.** At this time the country produced more iron than all the rest of the world.

◁ **An anchor being forged** in an ironworks foundry in about 1840.

▽ **Factories near the town of Wolverhampton** in 1866. The grime from the chimneys in blast furnaces, steel converters and mills changed the landscape so much that the area was known as the Black Country.

The iron industry had also grown with enormous speed. In 1740, British blast furnaces had made about 20,000 tonnes of 'pig iron' (iron ore crudely purified by heating). By the 1850s, they were making over 3.5 million tonnes a year. These huge supplies of iron were vital for building machines and other structures, such as bridges, ships and water pipes.

Ironworks, foundries and factories employed large numbers of people. Over a million men, women and children worked in the textile industry in the 1850s. One engineering works in Leeds employed over 500 people. But many, such as the craft workshops of master cutlers (knife-makers) in Sheffield, had only a handful of skilled workers.

▽ **The power and romance of industry** are shown in *Coal and Iron* – a painting of a scene in Tyneside, Tyne & Wear, by William Scott Bell from 1861.

MADE BY MACHINE

Machines lay at the heart of Britain's industrial growth. Since the 1760s, answers had been found to many problems, from spinning thread to printing newspapers. And a whole new industry had developed, which built and serviced these machines.

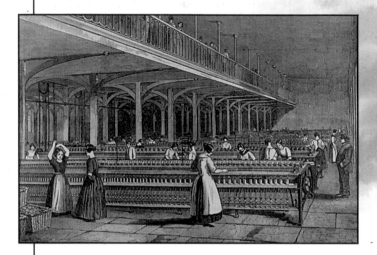

▷ (Above) **A blast furnace** at an ironworks in Birmingham. The molten metal is poured from the furnace and run into moulds.

△ **Workers in a cotton textile mill** in Lancashire in 1851. An average mill had at least 300 looms. The need for new machines boosted the engineering industry.

▷ **Workers build steam locomotives in a railway factory.** The railways grew at an amazing rate. By 1860, over 14,000 kilometres of track were in use.

A Victorian cotton mill was very noisy. All day long, the piston of the steam engine banged up and down, turning a giant wheel. Cogs and belts thundered as they carried this power to the factory floor where it drove the machines.

The 18th century 'spinning jenny' had allowed one worker to spin eight cotton threads at once. By the 1830s, one steam-powered 'mule', operated by a skilled worker, could produce more than 2,000 threads. These were woven into cloth on giant power looms.

◁ **The Machinery Hall at the Great Exhibition,** held in London in 1851. The Exhibition celebrated the progress achieved by industry. It contained over 13,000 marvellous machines, inventions, and modern products of all kinds. These included a steam hammer, cast bronze furniture and a collapsible piano for ships. All were on show in the Crystal Palace, a huge pavilion built of glass and iron. More than six million people visited the Exhibition.

Steam engines were also used in iron foundries. They powered the bellows which kept the fires roaring in the blast furnaces. These were loaded with iron ore and coke (baked coal). The iron melted and was poured out into moulds ('pigs'), leaving the impurities behind.

The iron could now be converted into an even tougher form, steel. 'Pig iron' was placed in a special container, and heated air was blown through it, burning away more impurities. This process, developed by Henry Bessemer in the 1850s, meant that for the first time steel could be made quickly and cheaply in large quantities.

Dozens of other machines were invented to shape and cut the metal. Some were huge, such as rolling mills or steam hammers. Others were small and delicate, such as the lathes used for cutting screw threads. These worked with great accuracy and could produce parts which were exactly the same.

△ **Two of Henry Bessemer's steel-converters** in an iron foundry. The converters were shaped like cement mixers and were tipped to pour out the molten steel. By 1871, over 750,000 people worked in metal-working, engineering and shipbuilding.

THE WORKERS

In 1841, there were 1.4 million people working on British farms. By 1901, the total was only 0.7 million. Farm machines had robbed many workers of their jobs, while enclosures had robbed them of land for growing food. Unemployed and landless, they swarmed to the towns to look for factory work.

Industrial towns grew with incredible speed. Glasgow, Birmingham and Bradford tripled in size during Victoria's reign. In the same period, the population of Middlesbrough rocketed from less than 400 to over 90,000.

▷ **A photograph of Longton,** a pottery town near Stoke-on-Trent, in about 1850. By this time, more people in England lived in towns than in the countryside.

△ **This cartoon by George Cruickshank** shows country people being put through a greedy boss's mincing machine and turned into factory 'hands'.

◁ **A cartoon showing the devil tempting a farmworker** to burn hayricks to protest about his lack of both work and money to feed his starving children and sick wife.

Houses for this flood of new workers were built hurriedly and cheaply. They stood in bleak rows, with narrow alleys between. They got little daylight and had no proper drains. A visitor to Leeds in 1841 was shocked by the workers' miserable living conditions. He noted "the wretched, stunted, decrepit and, frequently, the mutilated appearance of the broken-down labourers in the dirty, disagreeable streets".

Wages varied widely. In the 1850s a skilled craftsman might earn 40 shillings (£2.00) a week, but an unskilled child might get only five shillings (25p). The average wage was 15 shillings (75p).

When trade was bad, wages went down. In the early 1840s bad harvests and rising prices caused a serious slump. Print workers in Manchester had their weekly pay cut from 17 shillings (85p) to 6 shillings (30p). Many factories closed down and the labourers lost their jobs – and their pay packets.

△ **Terraced houses**, with chimneys and kilns at the back. The houses were built for factory workers in Sheffield.

◁ **The streets of a northern factory town**, overshadowed by tall chimneys and a railway viaduct. The terraced houses are small and cramped. Large families live in two rooms and a cellar. Few have anywhere to cook food.

BARRACLOUGH & TH

THE ALHAMBRA THEATRE

CHAINED TO THE MACHINE

"Whilst the engine runs, the people must work. The animal machine is chained fast to the iron machine, which knows no suffering and no weariness."
This was how one writer saw the grinding routine of each weekday in a Manchester cotton mill in early Victorian times.

The working week was a long one. By 1840 it lasted at least 12 hours a day, Monday to Friday. Saturday was a 'half-day' (9 hours), and the only full day off was Sunday (when many workers went to church in the morning). Here is the daily routine of a mill girl of 19:

5 a.m. Gets up and goes to work.
5.30 The steam engine starts turning the machinery and work begins.
7.30 A few minutes' break for cleaning the machine and grabbing a snack.
12.00 midday. Break for lunch: the girl must clean her machine before going home for food.
1 p.m. Back at work. No more breaks.
7 p.m. The engine stops. After cleaning her machine again, the girl goes home.

▽ **Young workers in a textile mill** in about 1860 weave cloth on power looms.

△ **Illustration from a book about factory life** published in 1830 to support the fight against the employment of children.

◁ **A Victorian room.**
Many of the products and materials here, including furniture, carpets and curtains, were factory made. Machines could turn out these goods cheaply, so that many middle-class people could afford them.

There was little time to rest. The workers had to keep up with the machines. Anyone who fell behind might be fined or even sacked by the factory owner. Those who got to work late suffered the same punishment.

Mills were kept very warm and damp, so that the cotton threads stayed strong. Workers wore very few clothes. When they left work in winter, they caught colds and lung infections.

△ **Mill workers in Wigan relax during their dinner hour.** This picture by Eyre Crowe was painted in 1874.

◁ (Far left) **Women at work in a cotton mill**. The boss and his overseer check samples of cloth. The air is thick with dust from the yarn, which got in everyone's hair and throats.

◁ **The Earl of Shaftesbury** inspects child workers in a mine.

BOSSES – GOOD AND BAD

Factory owners became part of the new, well-off middle classes. By 1851, there were over 85,000 of them. Most had small businesses, but many earned enough money to live in a fine house, own a private carriage and send their children to smart boarding schools.

A few factory owners grew especially powerful. The ironmasters of south Wales and mill owners of Lancashire formed committees to serve and further their interests. They became almost rulers of their local towns, with the people depending on them for jobs. As industry expanded, their wealth and power increased too. At Dowlais in south Wales, Sir John Guest employed 6,000 workers and had more than £1 million invested in his foundries.

▽ **The new town of Saltaire,** with its textile factory, was spacious and comfortable.

▽ **A wealthy mill owner and his family** look down proudly on the factories and grim houses below. Riches and success often opened up a gulf between the boss and his workers.

12

But not all employers were harsh taskmasters. Some realized that people worked better if they were happy and healthy. One of the earliest of these was Robert Owen, a mill owner in New Lanark in the 1820s. He reduced working hours, paid good wages and built comfortable houses for his workers. He also ran a school for the children.

In 1850, mill owner Sir Titus Salt moved his works from crowded Bradford into the open countryside and founded Saltaire. Here he built a large modern mill and surrounded it with 820 houses for his workers. Other owners followed Salt's example. In 1888, soap manufacturer William Lever built Port Sunlight in Merseyside. In 1893, George Cadbury founded the 'model village' of Bournville near Birmingham for the workers in his chocolate factory.

△ **On one side sits a fat, cigar-smoking boss.** On the other, his workers are so overworked and poorly paid that they have become skeletons. This cartoon highlights the terrible conditions in many 'sweatshops'.

△ **Sir Titus Salt** made his fortune making cloth from the wool of alpacas, domesticated llama-like animals from South America. In 1853, he built a new mill and 'model' town for his workers at Saltaire near Bradford.

△ **A sugar refinery of 1851**, where raw sugar cane is being 'refined' into pure sugar. The cane is being unloaded from horse-drawn carts.

◁ **Model homes** for workers, with verandas and a central courtyard, built in London.

13

CHILD LABOUR

If factory life was harsh for adults, it was even worse for children. Children were paid much less than grown-ups. In 1840, one Leeds mill owner paid children one-tenth of his men's wages. By the 1860s, children in the potteries were earning only 2/6d (equivalent to about 13 pence) for an 80-hour week.

△ **Classes at the Brook Street Ragged and Industrial School** in 1846.

Parents often had to send their children out to work so that they could earn a wage. In 1851, there were nearly five million children in Britain between the ages of three and 15. About 600,000 of these were forced to work for their living, either in factories and coal mines, or as servants.

The boys and girls (some of whom started work aged six or seven) were given the simpler and lighter jobs. But these could still be dangerous and very tiring. In cotton mills, child 'piecers' mended broken threads on the spinning frames, often crawling under the moving lines of thread to fix them or clear a blockage. In potteries, they turned the handle which kept the potter's wheel spinning, or carried clay moulds to be stacked in the ovens. In match factories, children worked with harmful chemicals. In coal mines, they pulled trucks underground, where there were rockfalls and poisonous gases.

▷ **Exhausted children at an evening lesson at their factory school.** Following the Factory Act of 1833 owners had to provide children with at least two hours' schooling each day. However, few children went. After a long day with little food, most fell asleep as soon as they got home.

△ **Children make matchboxes at home in 1871.** The pay was bad and the worker had to buy paste and string.

▷ **A factory inspector checks the ages of girls in a textile mill.** They look happy and well-fed.

Children were easier to control than adults, and mistakes or disobedience were punished by beatings. One child worker in the 1840s remembered being hit with a leather strap. Worse still: "I have been felled to the floor many times by the ruler, about 8 or 9 feet long, iron hoop at each end. For a time I could not tell whether I was living or dead."

△ **Miners at work in the Durham coalfields.** The boy on the right is the 'putter', whose job was to drive the pony and full wagon to the pit shaft. Even younger children worked as 'trappers'. They sat for hours in the dark, opening and shutting the traps, or doors, to let the wagons through and to allow stale air out and fresh air into the mine.

DANGER AND DISEASE

"Sheffield is one of the dirtiest and most smoky towns I ever saw ... One cannot be long there without experiencing the necessary inhalation of soot, which accumulates in the lungs." This was part of a report given to Parliament in 1843.

▷ **A Victorian painting of an iron foundry** by Eyre Crowe (1824-1910). The workers wear face masks and aprons, but no other special clothing to protect them against the heat and splashes of molten metal.

▽ **Smoke from the chimneys of pottery works in Stoke-on-Trent** was so thick that it blotted out the sunlight.

▷ **Women and children in the Glasgow slums, photographed in about 1868.** The alleys were narrow, dark and airless. A drain for water and sewage ran down the centre.

Inhaling (breathing in) soot from factory chimneys was only one of the dangers of working in an industrial area. Others were far greater. The Sheffield cutlers, grinding knives, worked in a cloud of fine metal dust which frequently caused lung disease. File-cutters and pottery workers were often poisoned by the lead dust which covered their hands (they seldom washed before eating).

As new products were developed, new processes were used. At first, no one realized how harmful these might be. Workers in match factories had their jaws eaten away by the chemical which coated the match-heads. Rubber- and bleach-making also used dangerous chemicals.

Workers in an engineering factory which made parts for the shipbuilding industry. There were cranes to shift the huge castings, but much of the hauling was done by muscle power. Such work was so hard, and the hours were so long, that most heavy labourers were worn out by the age of 50.

Mills and foundries spewed out a huge amount of filth into the environment. Dyes and other chemicals polluted rivers and lakes. Giant heaps of 'slag' (iron ore waste) surrounded mines and ironworks. Coal smoke belched into the sky, creating acid rain which killed grass and trees (the effects of acid rain were discovered as early as 1872). People who lived and worked in industrial towns also had to put up with crowded housing, poor food and bad drainage. Drinking water often came from the nearest rivers, which were full of germs. Many died young from diseases such as measles and typhoid. During the 1840s, over half of all children born in the slums of Glasgow died before the age of five.

A factory hand lies badly injured after being caught in a machine drive belt. The foreman tries to put on the brake. Workers often had limbs torn off in this kind of accident.

WORKING FOR REFORM

The factory system grew up so fast that there were few laws to control it. It was not until 1816 that Parliament ordered an inquiry into working conditions. The first factory act of 1819 limited the working hours of children under 16 to 12 hours a day.

Benjamin Disraeli

▷ **A poster of 1851 listing work rules to follow.** Here are the main Factory Acts and how they changed working conditions:
● **1833**
9-13 year olds could work up to only nine hours a day, with two hours schooling. 13-18 year olds could only work 12 hours a day (textile mills only).
● **1844**
Boys under 10 and women could not work in coal mines.

● **1847**
Children under 18 and women could work no more than 10 hours a day and up to only 58 hours a week.
● **1874**
Children under 10 could not work in textile mills.
● **1875**
Young boys could no longer work as chimney sweeps.
● **1878**
All previous laws concerning work are extended to cover other factories and workshops.

It was a small step. But gradually the process of reform quickened. Factory acts in 1833 and 1844 further reduced the working hours of young children in textile mills and mines. No-one under nine years old could now be employed. Factory inspectors were appointed by the government to check on the ages of workers and conditions of work. Dangerous machinery had to be covered by a protective guard. Then in 1847 came the Ten-Hour Act which set a limit to the length of the working day for women as well as children.

Many factory owners bitterly opposed these new laws. Some complained that reducing working hours would mean that fewer goods could be produced. This would lead to lower profits and higher prices. It would be more difficult to sell British goods abroad. But other employers led the movement for reform. Among them were John Fielden, a Yorkshire mill owner and Member of Parliament, and the Earl of Shaftesbury.

△ **The Earl of Shaftesbury.** He tried to reform conditions in mines, hospitals and factories.

◁ **Registering the unemployed** in London in 1887. There were no social security payments ('dole money') for those who were put out of work, and many unemployed people were penniless. They relied on 'soup kitchens' for food and on the distribution of clothes and boots, which were paid for by public charities.

These early reforms only applied to large textile mills and mines. Shaftesbury now tried to bring reforms to other parts of industry as well. One of the biggest problems was that the Ten-Hour Act was hard to enforce. Many bosses got round it by employing women in a relay system. They worked for a few hours at a time, never more than 10 in a day. Meanwhile the men still worked for up to 15 hours a day. It was not until 1874 that the government under Benjamin Disraeli pushed through a new law which fixed a 10-hour day for all workers.

◁ **Factory inspectors** study working conditions in a steelworks with its owners in the 1860s. When they were first appointed, in 1833, there were very few inspectors (only three for the whole of Yorkshire). They only had time to check on the larger factories. The hundreds of small workshops were seldom inspected, or even ignored altogether.

19

RISE OF THE UNIONS

Since the industrial age began, some workers had wanted to band together into unions. This would put them in a stronger position to fight for better working conditions. But there were laws stopping them from 'combining' into trade associations. These were called the Combination Laws.

▷ **Keir Hardie, the first socialist Member to be elected to Parliament** in 1892. His cloth cap shocked other MPs.

△ **The strike committee of women matchmakers.** In 1888 they went on strike for 12 days in protest at their conditions of work. They were paid only 4 shillings (20p) for a 60-hour week.

▽ **Soldiers fire on workers to control a miners' strike at Featherstone in 1893.** Miners in the north and Midlands went on strike for 15 weeks. This caused a disastrous shortage of coal.

In 1824 the Combination Laws were repealed (abolished). It was now legal to belong to a trade union. Unions sprang up among factory workers, builders and farm-workers.

In 1834 in London the reformer Robert Owen formed the Grand National Consolidated Trades Union. Its 400,000 or more members threatened to go on strike to demand an eight-hour working day. Parliament, factory owners and landowners were alarmed, and opposed the new unions. Yet, most of the early unions were badly run and had little money. They lasted only a short time.

Then, in 1851, a number of small and struggling engineering unions joined together to form the Amalgamated Society of Engineers (ASE). This was the first modern trade union. All members paid a weekly subscription of one shilling (5p). In return, the Society paid them money if they missed work through illness or went on strike, as well as benefit if they lost their jobs. The ASE soon had more than 11,000 members.

△ (Top) **Protesting union members march through the streets** during a strike. A new law in 1875 allowed them to 'picket' (discourage other workers from entering) their factory gates, as long as they did it peacefully.

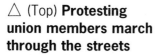

△ **The trade emblem** of the Amalgamated Society of Engineers.

In 1868 the trade unions held the first meeting of a joint Trades Union Congress (TUC) in Manchester. Three years later, Parliament passed the Trade Union Act which allowed unions to own property and raise funds.

By the 1890s there were more than 1.5 million trade union members. The unions began fighting for political power, and supported the new Labour Party.

△ **Dock workers vote by raising their hands** during their strike of 1889 to demand more pay. They got support from the public. The early trade unions had been for skilled craftsmen. It was not until the 1880s that the much bigger numbers of unskilled workers began to unite.

WORKSHOP OF THE WORLD

During Victoria's reign, Britain's population shot up from 18 million to more than 37 million. Despite the increase, people were better paid than ever before. This was largely because of the growth of industry, which brought higher wages and cheaper goods.

△ **Illustration from a tea caddy (box)** of a British company with plantations in Ceylon (now Sri Lanka).

◁ **British cargo ships,** small boats and local traders in the harbour at Calcutta, India, in 1880. The British built large docks here and at other major ports in the empire to handle the rapid increase in trade. Coaling stations were set up along the coasts of India and Africa to provide fuel for ships.

Production figures (millions of tonnes)
1830
Coal   20
Iron   8
Ships 111,000

1900
Coal   220
Iron   13
Ships 600,000+

△ **Figures showing how industrial production grew** during Victoria's reign.

This astonishing growth was made possible by a vast increase in the production of raw materials. The most important of these were iron and coal. Britain had huge reserves of these underground. As mining methods improved, they could be brought to the surface more quickly.

Britain began the age as the leader of what was called the Industrial Revolution. Her engineers and employers built the machines and factories which made possible the mass production of cheap goods. British railways and shipping could move these goods faster and further than any other kind of transport. But by the 1880s, the United States of America and Germany had caught up with Britain.

The growth of industry had changed daily life completely. The majority of workers now lived in towns. They worked together in huge groups in a tightly controlled environment ruled by the operation of machines.

GLOSSARY

bellows a container which is squeezed to force out air; generally used to make a fire burn fiercely.

blast furnace a furnace for melting iron ore which is heated using a blast of air.

converter a furnace designed to convert iron into steel.

cutler craftsman who makes knives, forks and other cutlery items.

dysentery an infection of the stomach, causing pain, diarrhoea and fever.

enclosures the fencing in of open common land with hedges and walls.

exports goods which are sold to foreign countries.

foundry a factory where metal ore is melted down, purified and moulded.

heavy industry the making of very large products, such as ships and locomotives.

impurities rock and other unwanted materials in a mineral ore.

ironmaster owner of an ironworks.

iron ore mined rock which contains iron.

kiln oven used to harden pottery by baking it at high temperatures.

lathe a machine which holds and turns a piece of wood or metal, so that it can be shaped precisely by a tool.

loom a machine which makes cloth by weaving threads together.

mule a spinning machine which makes more than one thread at a time.

overseer someone who watches over other people at work.

slump a sudden and serious fall in prices and business.

spinning jenny a spinning machine, invented in 1764.

textile a woven cloth or fabric.

typhoid an infection by bacteria transmitted in unclean water or food.

yarn a continuous strand made of fibres twisted together.

▷ **Map of Britain and Ireland** showing the location of places mentioned in this book, including the Places to Visit listed on page 2.

TIMECHART

1837 Victoria becomes queen.

1844 Third Factory Act (previous Acts in 1819 and 1833).

1847 Ten-Hour Act.

1851 Great Exhibition. First modern union (the ASE) formed.

1862 Royal Commission to investigate employment of young children.

1868 First Trades Union Congress.

1871 Trade unions legally recognized.

1874 Disraeli's Factory Act establishes 10-hour day.

1878 Disraeli's second Factory Act brings together previous measures.

1888 Port Sunlight founded by William Lever.

1892 Keir Hardie elected to Parliament.

1897 Act of Parliament allows workers to claim compensation for injury or disease at work.

1901 Death of Queen Victoria.

INDEX